Lent is a journey – travelling with Jesus as he returns from temptation in the wilderness to his victory over death on the cross in Jerusalem. Together we can make the journey through Lent together, knowing that Jesus journeys with us.

Index

To Lent or Not to Lent? ... *That Is the Question*

A good Lent can change your life, but it will be hard going. The self-examination of Lent does not come easily. We could pay lip service to Lent on a superficial level and let it slip by. We could treat Lent as just another date in the church calendar. Nothing changes for us and time marches on. However, if we go deeper and allow God to use Lent in our life, it will hurt, but we will be rewarded with the prize of having God come and dwell in our midst.

The Lenten journey is not for the faint hearted. If we are completely open to God this Lent, then expect hurt, expect pain. Our mediations and prayers through Lent will expose the fallacy of our identity constructs. A harsh light will shine on our narcissism, our vanity, our superficiality, and our hypocrisies, great and small. If after reading this you think that this does not apply to you then think again, as you have just demonstrated that it exactly applies to you.

During Lent, our vulnerabilities will be exposed. Above all, we will be shown how far we have wandered away from a living relationship with God and a Christ centred life. Fortunately, it does not end there with us broken and exposed. With God's grace and gentleness and with an open desire to change on our part, through our Lenten experience we are reconstructed in the image of Christ.

Lent can be a time of sacrifice, prayer, fasting, and reflection.

The Lent Detox - A Cleansing of Body, Mind & Spirit.

Lent can challenge us to grow spiritually. When we grow spiritually, our lives get healthier and stronger. We become more patient and caring at home, we become more integrity-filled and courageous at work and in our community. We become more resilient to face suffering and pain, we grow spiritually. This can impact us, and it follows, we can impact the world around us.

Goals For Lent

During Lent there is:

- **Increasing frequency and fervency of our prayers** — through a focus of consistent prayer during the Lenten season we come closer to God.
- **A Growing desire to connect with Jesus** — through greater reflection on what Jesus has achieved for us we connect with Jesus and grow more in his image.
- **A Deepening dissatisfaction with what the world has to offer** — through experiencing the greater joy of walking closely with God we turn our back on worldly things and turn our whole being towards living a fulling Christian life.
- **Expanding habits of generosity** — through practicing the joy of giving to the church and beyond we show generosity and in doing so we experience God's benevolence.
- **Surging distaste with sins that normally go ignored** — through intentional reflection on areas that need repentance we examine those areas of our life that is a block to strengthening our Christian faith.
- **Swelling faith that relies on God instead of on self-medication through food or screens** — through fasting from some of our typical comforts we recognise the hold they have on us and when ourselves of their destructive control of our life.
- **Hungering deeply for the things of God** — through redirecting our appetites toward Jesus.
- **Escalating courage to face a hostile world with boldness** — through prayer and joy to embrace the hope of presented by Easter.

What is a Lent devotional?
Any Lent devotional is simply an invitation to reflect on God's presence and movement in our personal lives through this season. During Lent, let us open our minds and hearts to the transforming power of God's presence and grace. We try to empty ourselves of our self-righteousness and pride and see how we can respond to God's call in new ways by placing ourselves in God's hands. Through God's transforming power we will bring deep hope into our own lives and our world. The journey begins…

Preparing For Lent

Sunday before Ash Wednesday

There is a saying: 'The first step is the hardest...' Have you ever found this? Especially if the journey is a difficult one; one that you don't really want to do perhaps, or one that is scary or unpleasant. The best way to combat these negative thoughts is to plan for the journey so that it does not seem so daunting.

Plans for Lent

Sit, think, pray, and write down what you want from your Lent journey and what you think God wants for you from Lent.

What are my Lent Goals?

This Lent think about:
Fasting from selfishness and be compassionate to others.
Fasting from anger and be filled with patience.
Fasting from sadness and be filled with gratitude.
Fasting from worries and trust in God.
Fasting from complaining and be positive.
Fasting from pressures and be prayerful.
Fasting from pessimism and be filled with hope.
Fasting from bitterness and forgive yourself and others.
Fasting from grudges and be reconciled.
Fasting from words and be quiet so you can listen.
Fasting from hurting words and be kind.

Prayer for the start of Lent
Lord, as I start preparing for my journey through Lent, please show me what I should be focusing on and what is irrelevant.

Loving God, help me to grow in faith and love over these next days of Lent, and may I be brought even closer to you in my life. Lord, you are my God, and I am yours, may I never veer from the perfect path which you have set before me. Please be my rock and my strength.

Almighty and ever living God, you invite me deeper into your world during Lent.

May this time be one of outward focus; seeking you in people and things I often ignore.

Help me live a Lent focused on you and what you have to say to me and what you have to show me.

Give me a heart hungry to serve you and those who need what I have to give.

Monday before Ash Wednesday

What is Lent about?

Many spend the time in self-examination and reflection as modelled by Jesus in Matthew 4: 1-11 where he prayed and fasted for 40 days before beginning his ministry.

What happened during those 40 days of fasting and praying in the wilderness? Maybe Jesus needed some time with God to sort through the major changes happening in his life. Maybe he needed a break from family, friends, and his regular routine in order to see God and himself more clearly. Maybe he sought more time with God as he searched for direction and answers to the question that we, too have from time to time: "Who am I called to be?" During Lent we, too are invited into this time of introspection.

Lent's ever-present question is 'what shall we give up for Lent?' but there is an alternative option: 'What shall we do this Lent?'

Pray

This lent, loving God, be by my side through the good times and hard times. Let me be honest and true as I enter a time of self-examination and reflection. Please help me to see myself and my relationships more clearly. Please show me the areas of my life that displease you and are blocking my relationship with you. Please show those areas of my life that please you and bring me closer to you. Please show me who am I called to be?

Shrove Tuesday

Joel 2:12-14
"Even now," declares the Lord, "return to me with all your heart, with fasting and weeping and mourning."

Rend your heart and not your garments. Return to the Lord your God, for he is gracious and compassionate, slow to anger and abounding in love....

Today is the last day before Lent and a time in which we repent for our sins and turn away from our destructive patterns. In order to do that, we must understand and admit those sins and patterns, which is why this day is sometimes called Shrove Tuesday from an old word meaning 'forgiveness.'

Lent Spiritual Prompt
Write down the good things in your life that God has given to you.
Write down the things in your life that pleases God.
Write down the things in your life that does not please God.

Prayer For Lent
Thank you loving God for the gift of this season of Lent. Thank you for drawing me into a closer relationship with you throughout the coming days of Lent. Please walk with me in my wilderness during Lent.

May these weeks leading up to Good Friday and the glory of Resurrection Sunday remind me of who you are and how you love me.

May I walk through this season intentionally, please remove distractions that take my gaze away from your glory. Show me what is in my life that pleases you and show me those aspects of my life that I need to change.

Lent begins

- **Ash Wednesday**

Genesis 3.19
You are dust, and to dust you shall return.

Ash Wednesday is the beginning of Lent. As the ash is placed on our foreheads in the shape of the cross, those words from Genesis are spoken: "Remember you are dust, and to dust you shall return." It is a day to lament our disconnectedness from God. It begins a time where we consider those failures in our own lives which separate us from God. The sign of the cross reminds us that in Jesus, our failure is overcome by his resurrection. We can use Lent to meet with God and ask God to bridge the distance we put between him and us.

Lent Spiritual Prompt
As humans we all fail, in some way, every day. Ask yourself honestly where have you failed in your Christian faith? If you have no answer now, then roll this question over in your mind during the coming days of Lent and try to answer it before the end of Lent.

Prayer for Lent
During this Lent please God bring me closer to you.
Please God show me those failures in my life that separates me from you.
Please God show me how to bridge the distance between us.
May I be at peace this Lent, may I surrender what has been burdensome to you this Lent, may I repent and turn back to you.

Thursday after Ash Wednesday

Matthew 11:28 'Come to me, all you who are weary and burdened...'

Quiet prayer is a time to rest and wait in God's presence, it is a time to listen and receive. As we draw close to God, He promises to draw close to us. We can be deeply encouraged, strengthened, and healed as we take time to be still before God.

Prayer Spotlight
During Lent lift up specific requests to God:
Pray for your family.
Pray for opportunities to share your faith.
Pray for opportunities to love and serve others.

Prayer For Lent

During this Lent please God bring me closer to you.

May I quiet the noise that pulls me from you and attracts my attention on lesser things.

May I see your goodness and your glory in new ways throughout this season of Lent.

May I know the depths of your love for me more fully.
Draw me closer to you, that I might know you better and understand you more completely.

Changes for Lent

Lent Reflections

Friday after Ash Wednesday

Isaiah 55 'Come, all you who are thirsty, come to the waters ... listen, listen to me ...'

Psalm 37 'Rest in the Lord, and wait patiently for Him...'

Lent Spiritual Prompt
What part does humility play in your daily life and actions?
What steps can you take to make sure your words and actions are motivated by a desire to serve and help others rather than seek attention and praise for yourself?

Prayer for Lent
I pray that Lent, for me, is not just about giving things up or taking things on, but that I would give you glory through Lent, Lord.
May my actions reflect You, and may I worship You through all that I say and do throughout the weeks to come.
May my praise for You never cease in this season.
May my worship be unending.
May this season of Lent bring new hope and new healing to me.

Saturday after Ash Wednesday

What to Give Up . . .

Give up complaining . . .
          . . . focus on gratitude.
Give up pessimism . . .
          . . . become an optimist.
Give up harsh judgments . . .
          . . . think kindly thoughts.
Give up worry . . .
          . . . trust Divine Providence.
Give up discouragement . . .
          . . . be full of hope.

Give up bitterness . . .
    . . . turn to forgiveness.
Give up hatred . . .
    . . . return good for evil.
Give up negativism . . .
    . . . be positive.
Give up anger . . .
    . . . be more patient.
Give up pettiness . . .
    . . . become mature.
Give up gloom . . .
    . . . enjoy the beauty that is all around you.
Give up jealousy . . .
    . . . pray for trust.
Give up gossiping . . .
    . . . control your tongue.
Give up sin . . .
    . . . turn to virtue.
Give up giving up . . .
    . . . hang in there!

Lent Spiritual Prompt

Think of a person with whom you have a strained relationship and make some gesture toward improving that relationship.

Pray

Direct my actions, Lord, by your holy inspiration and carry them forward by your gracious help, that all my works may begin in you and by you be happily ended.

You know my strained relationships. I pray about this now. Please grant me insight and courage. Help me to make amends.

Please forgive me so that I may forgive others.

Forgiveness

Thoughts & Prayers

First Sunday of

The Spiritual Desert Experience

Sunday

Mark 1:12–14
The Spirit sent him out into the wilderness, and he was in the wilderness for forty days, being tempted by Satan. He was with the wild animals, and angels attended him.

James 1:3 The testing of your faith produces perseverance.

As we step into Lent, we are reminded that Jesus spent forty days in the wilderness before starting His ministry.

Throughout scripture we read of many characters who experienced the wilderness, usually before they stepped into a significant calling.

We all walk through wilderness times, those spiritually dry places where God teaches us to trust Him. It's often in the middle of the bleakest desert that God heals us and sets us free from false narratives that hold us captive.

Lent Spiritual Prompt
Why do you think the Spirit led Jesus out into the wilderness to be tempted?
In the desert of daily routine can you learn to find value in the humblest tasks?

Pray

Father, you've led me to this wilderness to heal me, change me, and reveal yourself to me. I trust in your plan for me as well as your willingness and ability to provide for me here. I don't want to grumble. I want to thank you for all the gifts you have given me. Whatever happens to me in life, dear Lord, even when the road is rocky and leads me through wild or frightening passes, help me to hold on tight to you.

Thank you for the endurance and courage of Jesus, and his steadfastness in temptation. May I learn from him, may my faith in him never fail, and may I grow more like him as I follow – slowly, stumblingly – after him. Amen.

Monday

Deuteronomy 2:7
The Lord your God has blessed you in all the work of your hands. He has watched over your journey through this vast wilderness. These forty years the Lord your God has been with you, and you have not lacked anything.

All sorts of things can lead us to a barren, wilderness place and our days can often feel long, dark, and extremely difficult – physically, emotionally, or spiritually. Maybe you find yourself in a place where everything feels as though it is being stripped away and you hunger and thirst for something more. Tell God about it.

Lent Spiritual Prompt

Can you describe a time in your life that you would identify as "wilderness"?
Have you ever encountered a wilderness experience? A place where perhaps you found yourself discouraged, uncertain, tired, weary, and fed-up.

Pray

Loving God let me tell you about my wilderness experience.
Father, you've led me to this wilderness to heal me, change me, and reveal yourself to me. I trust in your plan for me as well as your

willingness and ability to provide for me here.

I don't want to wander in fear and unbelief. Help me believe you have freedom for me on the other side of this wilderness.

I don't want to self-protect, isolate, or place my heart high on a shelf out of reach. I want to bring you my whole heart. I want to uncover so you can cover and heal. I want to hold nothing back, Jesus. I don't want to doubt your love. I want to grow deeper in my understanding of your love for me, but I know I need your help to even grasp how long, how wide, and how deep your love truly is.

Glory To God

I am Grateful For

Tuesday

Deuteronomy 8:2
Remember how the Lord your God led you all the way in the wilderness these forty years, to humble and test you in order to know what was in your heart, whether or not you would keep his commands.

Wilderness wanderers usually know what it is to feel lonely and hopeless; disillusionment, discouragement and a sense of abandonment can so easily set in as we seek ways to get out of our desolate place. It is a natural human emotion to cry out for help and relief, to long for such days in the desert place to cease. The Hebrew word for 'desert' means 'place of speaking'. When we feel abandoned, God always finds a way to reassure us of His presence and speak to us.

Lent Spiritual Prompt
Can you recall times of struggle or drought where you also experienced moments of encouragement or felt close to God? Did you believe God "watched over your journey through this vast wilderness." Deuteronomy 2:7

Pray
Gracious God, you've led me to this wilderness to heal me, change me, and reveal yourself to me. I trust in your plan for me as well as your willingness and ability to provide for me here.
I don't want to doubt your presence. You've led me here to reveal yourself to me. You are helping me exercise my spiritual muscles in discerning your voice in new ways.
Loving God, I struggle to hear that gentle whisper you're teaching me to listen for. Open my eyes to recognise you in the ordinary as well as in the extraordinary.

Wednesday

Psalm 63:1
You, God, are my God, earnestly I seek you; I thirst for you, my

whole being longs for you, in a dry and parched land where there is no water.

Though we try to avoid the desert experience, God leads us to the wilderness to reveal Himself to us in new and life-giving ways. The wilderness calls us to be still, reflect, pray, wrestle, and to listen to God. Our wilderness experience tends to bring to the surface what is happening deep within us, and it is possible that we find ourselves, similarly to Jesus, being prepared for what lies ahead.

The desert experience lays bare our inner emptiness, detaches us, and can simplify a person's life down to the bare essentials. In the spiritual desert we are confronted by all our baggage and dark spots. We resist going into the silence and quiet because we do not like what we see there.

Desert time is vital to a mature relationship with God. If we are committed in our faith, then God is going to bring us to the desert at some point to look deeply at ourselves and see ourselves the way God sees us. This means we will have to confront the dark spots of our lives and the things we do our best to hide from God and from the rest of the world.

Lent Spiritual Prompt
Do I acknowledge my complete dependence on God?
Do I trust the power and presence of God in my life?
Do I prefer the easy way, the path of least resistance and the most gratification?
Do I value money, time, and prestige more than people?

Pray
Gracious God, you have led me to this wilderness to heal me, change me, and reveal yourself to me. I trust in your plan for me as well as your willingness and ability to provide for me here.
Quiet my heart to hear your voice. Father, I don't want to resist your will and your timing. Help me lay down my agenda and my pride. Teach me submission and humility. Let me know your present as I wander in this wilderness.

Thursday

2 Corinthians 12:9
"My grace is sufficient for you, for power is made perfect in weakness."

Jesus' time in the desert prepared him to begin his public ministry. When we confront our demons with God's help, we are stronger. It is in the desert time—our time of prayer, solitude, and aloneness with God—that God readies us for our next steps.

The wilderness can be seen as a beautiful and necessary part of the earth's life. We can see the wilderness as a metaphor. We all need breathing space, time to just be, peace and quiet, and the opportunity to retreat, regroup, and get a better perspective on life.

Lent Spiritual Prompt
Have you found spiritual growth or healing in your spiritual desert?

As we continue on our Lenten journey, let me be led by the Spirit to have the courage to deal with the desert as Jesus did. I pray that during these weeks of Lent, God will strengthen me in my weakness the way Jesus was strengthened.

Pray
Lord, you've led me to this wilderness to heal me, change me, and reveal yourself to me. I trust in your plan for me as well as your willingness and ability to provide for me.

I pray that in the wilderness you never leave me alone. Please be with me and let your light shine on my path so I can see the way and never be lost in the wilderness.

Gracious God, let me be led by the Spirit to have the courage to deal with the desert as Jesus did. I pray that during these weeks of Lent, God will strengthen me in my weakness the way Jesus was strengthened.

What ARE You Thankful for?

Wandering in the Wilderness

Friday

Ecclesiastes 3:1 "There is a time for everything, and a season for every activity under the heavens."

To be led by the Spirit requires listening and obedience to God. The wilderness can be seen as a situation of austerity – a desert place offering no luxury. Intimidating, disheartening, and downright dangerous, time in the wilderness is daunting and not something to look forward to. It's a place where survival skills are called for. Metaphorically, it is about loneliness or depression, about adversity – maybe bereavement, tough times.

Desert time can be associated with time for solitude. Time alone can be renewing and recharging, a dedicated opportunity for reflection and prayer, a time for us to see more clearly and to put our struggles into proper perspective. It is important to go to the desert to come closer to God.

The desert journey can be a time of learning to know and to trust God, but also an increase in self-knowledge. The desert time gives us a deepening awareness of our thoughts. We can never fully escape our struggles and temptations—time alone reminds us often it is our own thoughts and behaviours that are our biggest obstacles to having a closer relationship with God.

Lent Spiritual Prompt
What are the thoughts and behaviours that are your biggest obstacles to having a closer relationship with God? What is Jesus saying to you about the necessity of desert experience for your inner life? How do you build in and practice some desert time in your live?

Pray
Father, you've led me to this wilderness to heal me, change me, and reveal yourself to me. I trust in your plan for me as well as your willingness and ability to provide for me here.
Gracious God, help me to build in and practice some desert time in my spiritual life. Help me to learn to know you and trust you. Let

this desert time deepen my awareness of you and your direction for me. Show me the obstacles in my life that are blocking my relationship with you.

Saturday

Luke 5:16 "But Jesus often withdrew to the wilderness for prayer."

The wilderness can also be a place of formation and a place of preparation. The Israelites took a census and got organized during their time in the wilderness. John the Baptist was a voice crying out from the wilderness. Jesus spent 40 days fasting in the wilderness before beginning his public ministry. Once Christ began healing and teaching, people followed him everywhere, but he often withdrew to the wilderness for prayer.

In our spiritual desert experience, there is time and space to think and pray.

The desert has things to teach us. We see the careful provision of our Father in a different light. His love stands out in stark relief against the background of the desert's barren landscape. In the wilderness, we come to the end of ourselves. We learn in new and deeper ways to cling to Him and wait for Him.

When we come out of the desert, the desert lessons stay with us. We take them with us into the next stretch of our Christian journey. We remember the God who led us through the desert, and we know that He is with us still. Desert times are fruitful times. Though they seem barren, lush fruit is being produced in our lives when we walk through the desert. The Lord will sanctify our desert times and make them to be fruitful in our life.

Lent Spiritual Prompt
What have you learnt this week about the desert experience?

One thing is clear in Scripture: We are never alone in the wilderness. If you are walking through a wilderness of your own, pray to be reminded of the promise that God will never leave or forsake you.

Pray
Father, you've led me to this wilderness to heal me, change me, and reveal yourself to me. I trust in your plan for me as well as your willingness and ability to provide for me here.

Dear Lord, I know that wherever I am, You are with me—guiding, protecting, providing. You make streams flow in the desert; You cause a root to grow out of dry ground. Thank You for giving me the opportunity to see You work when all hope seems lost.

I know I am never alone in the wilderness. I pray to be reminded of the promise that God will never leave or forsake me.

In my wilderness experience show me that desert times are fruitful times. Let me have faith to know that though this time seems barren, lush fruit is being produced in my life when I walk with God through this desert. Please Lord sanctify my desert time and make it to be fruitful in my life.

- **Second Week of Lent**

Second Sunday of

Sunday

John 15 – Jesus says, '...if you abide in me and I in you, you will bear much fruit; apart from me, you can do nothing ...'

During Lent, perhaps we might enter a place where we rediscover our sense of belonging to our Creator, to each other, irrespective of colour, culture, or creed. This Lent we should strive to name and own our ambitions, including the temptations that stand in the way of us achieving God's plan for us.

Pray

Loving God, challenge me when I talk of anyone as less than myself, and help me speak up when others speak in ways that diminish or disparage people who differ from them. Grant me patience to listen to you to discern your plan for me. Let me abide in you and let me bear fruit for you.

Monday

Philippians 2:4
Let each of you look not only to his own interests, but also to the interests of others.

Acts 20:35
In all things I have shown you that by working hard in this way we must help the weak and remember the words of the Lord Jesus, how he himself said, 'It is more blessed to give than to receive.'"

When we see a person who is homeless, we have the opportunity to pray for them and ask for God's protection to cover them.

The next time you pass a person who has no home, pray for them.

Pray

Loving God, I pray for the people I have passed sleeping in doorways. Show me what I should do to help change their situations. I pray for transforming hearts and minds to foster generosity and compassion toward all those who have no homes and who are in need. Inspire those with resources and power to be Your hands and feet, extending Your love to those in need.

Forgiveness During Lent

Fears

Tuesday

Philippians 2:3–4
Do nothing from selfish ambition or conceit, but in humility count others more significant than yourselves. Let each of you look not only to his own interests, but also to the interests of others.

The world is too much with us; late and soon,
Getting and spending, we lay waste our powers.
Wordsworth

The pursuit of success is the dominant narrative of our time, where social media encourages us to present a perfect image of our lives with the drive towards a bigger house, better job, or flashier holiday.

Much of what society teaches us, particularly in western society, is to focus on the wrong things. So many people end up making themselves ill and tired hustling to get those things. Sometimes people actually get those things, and it does not make them happy. Or in the process of striving, they neglect the things that truly make them happy.

Lent Spiritual Prompt
Talk to God about your life goals and your decisions. What "material things" are controlling your life? List them and ask the Holy Spirit to help you release control and let them go, so that God's perfect will is done in your life. At your core are you content and at peace with your life? If not, talk to someone you trust about this.

Pray
Gracious God, please help me to spend my time, talents, and assets wisely. Please break the bondage of conspicuous consumption over our nation and over me. Help me to be a better steward of the resources You have blessed me with. Holy Spirit, please help me to be more disciplined with my lifestyle. Loving God, help me to learn to be content with what I have instead of wanting more. Help those who are in financial trouble. Many need a miracle in their finances, and I ask for Your intervention.

Compassionate God, please forgive me for greed, selfish ambition, idolatry, conceit, and arrogance. Forgive me for loving things and placing them over You. Forgive me for not being a good steward of Your blessings. I renounce any gods of materialism. Lord, remind me of those I need to forgive; and help me to forgive.

Wednesday

Be silent.
Be still.
Alone
Empty
Before your God
Say nothing.
Ask nothing.
Be silent.
Be still.
Let your God
Look upon you.
That is all
God knows.
Understands
Loves you with
An enormous love
God only wants to
Look upon you
With Love
Quiet
Still

Be
Let your God
Love you.

Thursday

1 Timothy 6:11–12
11 But you, man of God, flee from all this, and pursue righteousness, godliness, faith, love, endurance, and gentleness. 12 Fight the good fight of the faith. Take hold of the eternal life to which you were called.

What do want from life? Success? Money?
There are plenty of studies that show that after a certain point, more money doesn't make us happier; but it can't deny that money can remove common sources of unhappiness. While there is nothing wrong with wanting more in our career and life, we should caution ourselves and ask: Where does that desire come from? "Is it from a place of lack or a place of fullness?" Success is no assurance of happiness or contentment. It can be a barrier in our Christian life.

Lent Spiritual Prompt
Take a moment to define success not as the world defines it but how it should be defined in our Christian life?

Pray
Gracious God, you know me so well. Relieve me of those desires that I think will me make happy but in reality, will damage and hurt me. Let me focus on you and show me what I should be pursuing in my life.

Friday

Romans 8:6
The mind governed by the flesh is death, but the mind governed by the Spirit is life and peace.

Allowing God into the pain in our life is very simple but very powerful. It can help us change the trajectory of our life. Take time this Lent to think about sharing money, time, and gifts, discovering how we can build a community of love through our many acts of service.

The sacrifice of God is a broken spirit; a broken and contrite heart God will not despise. Let us come to God, who is full of compassion, ready to listen and forgive.

I list those things that are blocking me from having a closer relationship with God.

Still my heart and mind as I come into God's presence.

Pray
Loving God thank you for your love and care for me. I want my thoughts to be governed by you. Please grant me peace. Show me how to get release. I submit my thoughts to you. Please overcome the darkness in my life that is making me miserable. Please let me be free and healthy. Show me how I may be of service to you.

Saturday

My dear brothers and sisters, take note of this: Everyone should be quick to listen, slow to speak, and slow to become angry (James 1:19).

"In your anger do not sin" Do not let the sun go down while you are still angry, and do not give the devil a foothold (Ephesians 4:26-27).

But now you must also rid yourselves of all such things as these: anger, rage, malice, slander, and filthy language from your lips (Colossians 3:8).

Do not be quickly provoked in your spirit, for anger resides in the lap of fools (Ecclesiastes 7:9).

Is there something in your life that is worrying you and has taken over your life? You don't seem to talk about anything except this. Has it become a nightmare? It doesn't go away; you live and breathe it? Is there something that has cast a long shadow of unhappiness over your life?

Are you liable to fester all day about a stranger's rudeness?

We live in such an incredibly divided world at the moment, and everyone seems very quick to judge. When someone cuts you up in their car, or pushes in front of you, choose an empathetic thought. Perhaps they've had a terrible night with a loved one being sick. Choose the narrative that stops you feeling tension and frustration.

When we are faced with a festering annoyance, let God challenge us to try and take another path in thought and action.

Pray
The Merton Prayer

My Lord God,
I have no idea where I am going.
I do not see the road ahead of me.
I cannot know for certain where it will end.

Nor do I really know myself, and the fact that I think I am following your will does not mean that I am actually doing so.

But I believe that the desire to please you does in fact please you.

And I hope I have that desire in all that I am doing.

I hope that I will never do anything apart from that desire.

And I know that if I do this, you will lead me by the right road, though I may know nothing about it.

Therefore, will I trust you always though I may seem to be lost and in the shadow of death.

I will not fear, for you are ever with me, and you will never leave me to face my perils alone.

Thomas Merton

- **Third Week of Lent**

Third Sunday of

Sunday

Isaiah 40:8 "The grass withers and the flowers fall, but the word of our God endures forever."

Making a virtue out of necessity.

How are you doing today?
How did you sleep last night?
Are you content with your life?

Take time today to list the good things in your life. All those things that you are thankful for and that add colour to your daily existence.

On the radio recently a woman talked about how she was born into a family where her father was an alcoholic and her mother had Asperger's Syndrome. Life as a child was difficult. The woman developed resilience and a strong Christian faith. Often, she would ask God why he had given her these parents instead of a nice comfortable family.

Through prayer and being open to God, the woman came to understand that God had not given her to these parents for them to look after her, but instead, God had given to her these parents for her to care for them.

Through the experience of caring for her parents as a child, the woman developed resilience and skills that as an adult she was able to use to serve God and aid others.

That understanding and acceptance gave her peace and an understanding to get on with her life and not dwell on what might have been.

"Some of you have been in deep waters through pain, poverty, and bereavement. Loved ones and friends have forsaken you – but not God. He will hear the prayer of the humble heart. God will not forsake you. He is near in your distress." — Charles Spurgeon

Pray

Lord, remind me how You are my refuge and strength at all times. Please grant me understanding and insight into this situation I am in. Let me have the faith to know that you will not forsake me and that are near. Please give me peace in the assurance that you are my refuge and my strength. There are there beside me in my trouble.

Psalm 46:1-3
God is our refuge and strength, a very present help in trouble. Therefore, we will not fear though the earth gives way, though the mountains be moved into the heart of the sea, though its waters roar and foam, though the mountains tremble at its swelling.

Monday

In the book, 'David and Goliath: Underdogs, Misfits, and the Art of Battling Giants,' Malcolm Gladwell discusses the big fish in the little pond theory. During Lent you were able to record the things in your life that please God, but perhaps there is an ache in your life where you think you have failed or missed a chance. A road you failed to take or one that was barred to you from taking. Perhaps an ambition was thwarted. Maybe this is an ache you have carried for some time and each time you examine it, there is hurt like a knock against a bruise. Try now to re-examine that ache in a different light.

In his book, Gladwell presents a large amount of data that demonstrates how being a big fish in a little pond can be just as, if not more, advantageous than being a little fish in a big pond.

Gladwell explains the "Big Fish-Little Pond Effect" as follows: 'The more elite an educational institution is, the worse students feel about their own academic abilities . . . And that feeling — as subjective and ridiculous and irrational as it may be — matters.'

How do you feel about your abilities — this can shape your willingness to tackle challenges and finish difficult tasks. It's a crucial element in your motivation and confidence. It could be blocking the work that God wants you to do.

Look again at that road not taken in your life. Realistically examine how it would have changed things both in a positive and negative way.

Pray
Dear God, as I look back on my life and look back on the choices I have made and those that were made for me, help to find peace, hope and acceptance. Let me accept what has been and find the strength and grace to forgive and move on. Show me how to use my time and talents for your glory.

Tuesday

Over the next few days, we are going to examine and reflect on the David and Goliath story. Your eyes are probably glazing over, and you are thinking borrrrring. Bear with this. You might find something in it that rings a bell in your own life.

David and Goliath
1 Samuel 17

Now the Philistines gathered their forces for war and assembled at Sokoh in Judah. They pitched camp at Ephes Dammim, between Sokoh and Azekah. 2 Saul and the Israelites assembled and camped in the Valley of Elah and drew up their battle line to meet the Philistines. 3 The Philistines occupied one hill and the Israelites another, with the valley between them.

4 A champion named Goliath, who was from Gath, came out of the Philistine camp. His height was six cubits and a span. [a] 5 He had a bronze helmet on his head and wore a coat of scale armour of bronze weighing five thousand shekels[b]; 6 on his legs he wore bronze greaves, and a bronze javelin was slung on his back. 7 His spear shaft was like a weaver's rod, and its iron point weighed six hundred shekels. [c] His shield bearer went ahead of him.

8 Goliath stood and shouted to the ranks of Israel, "Why do you come out and line up for battle? Am I not a Philistine, and are you not the servants of Saul? Choose a man and have him come down to me. 9 If he is able to fight and kill me, we will become your subjects; but if I overcome him and kill him, you will become our subjects and serve us." 10 Then the Philistine said, "This day I defy the armies of Israel! Give me a man and let us fight each other." 11 On hearing the Philistine's words, Saul and all the Israelites were dismayed and terrified.

Footnotes
a1 Samuel 17:4 That is, about 9 feet 9 inches or about 3 meters.
b1 Samuel 17:5 That is, about 125 pounds or about 58 kilograms.
c1 Samuel 17:7 That is, about 15 pounds or about 6.9 kilograms.

Think of some world issues where there is a David and Goliath situation?
Think about your life and those around you. Is there a David and Goliath situation there?

Pray
Gracious God, I pray for those countries that are being bullied and attacked by bigger and stronger nations. Let your justice intervene.

Gracious God, I pray about this personal situation where a big bully is causing fear and hurt. Let your justice intervene.

Wednesday

David and Goliath
1 Samuel 17

12 Now David was the son of an Ephrathite named Jesse, who was from Bethlehem in Judah. Jesse had eight sons, and in Saul's time he was very old. 13 Jesse's three oldest sons had followed Saul to the war: The firstborn was Eliab; the second, Abinadab; and the third, Shammah. 14 David was the youngest. The three oldest followed Saul, 15 but David went back and forth from Saul to tend his father's sheep at Bethlehem.

16 For forty days the Philistine came forward every morning and evening and took his stand.

17 Now Jesse said to his son David, "Take this ephah[d] of roasted grain and these ten loaves of bread for your brothers and hurry to their camp. 18 Take along these ten cheeses to the commander of their unit. See how your brothers are and bring back some assurance[e] from them. 19 They are with Saul and all the men of Israel in the Valley of Elah, fighting against the Philistines."

20 Early in the morning David left the flock in the care of a shepherd, loaded up and set out, as Jesse had directed. He reached the camp as the army was going out to its battle positions, shouting the war cry. 21 Israel and the Philistines were drawing up their lines facing each other. 22 David left his things with the keeper of supplies, ran to the battle lines, and asked his brothers how they were.

Footnotes
d1 Samuel 17:17 That is, probably about 36 pounds or about 16 kilograms.
e1 Samuel 17:18 Or some token; or some pledge of spoils

David does not know what lies in front of him. He is obedient. His humble job of tending to the sheep taught him skills that he was soon to put to great use. He is an expert in protecting the sheep from wild animals and is proficient in the use of a sling.

Prayer for strength and comfort
I know I am weak, Lord, so I will allow you to carry me through this valley. I struggle to think clearly, so I depend upon your living word to lift me. I feel such darkness around, so I look to your light.

I walk with a heavy heart, so I will give you each burden. I wonder if my heart can take the strain, so I rest in your love and peace. I think of a candle to remind me of the warm glow of your hope in dark places. Teach me to be obedient. Amen.

Bible Verses

Thursday

David and Goliath
1 Samuel 17

23 As he was talking with them, Goliath, the Philistine champion from Gath, stepped out from his lines and shouted his usual defiance, and David heard it.

24 Whenever the Israelites saw the man, they all fled from him in great fear.

25 Now the Israelites had been saying, "Do you see how this man keeps coming out? He comes out to defy Israel. The king will give great wealth to the man who kills him. He will also give him his daughter in marriage and will exempt his family from taxes in Israel."

26 David asked the men standing near him, "What will be done for the man who kills this Philistine and removes this disgrace from Israel? Who is this uncircumcised Philistine that he should defy the armies of the living God?"

27 They repeated to him what they had been saying and told him, "This is what will be done for the man who kills him."

28 When Eliab, David's oldest brother, heard him speaking with the men, he burned with anger at him and asked, "Why have you come down here? And with whom did you leave those few sheep in the wilderness? I know how conceited you are and how wicked your heart is; you came down only to watch the battle."

29 "Now what have I done?" said David. "Can't I even speak?" 30 He then turned away to someone else and brought up the same matter, and the men answered him as before. 31 What David said was overheard and reported to Saul, and Saul sent for him.

According to Malcolm Gladwell in 'David and Goliath: Underdogs,

Misfits, and the Art of Battling Giants' there are medical experts who believe that Goliath was suffering from acromegaly, which causes rapid, excess, and abnormal growth. It has a side effect of causing restrictive sight. Goliath, in the biblical story, needs someone to lead him out and he has to get close to David to see him. Perhaps an indication of poor sight.

Although, it would appear, David does not stand a chance against this giant, Goliath, once you start factoring in that Goliath is weighted down with heavy armour, is slow and may have limited vision the situation takes on a different perspective.

Sometimes by talking through a challenging situation and considering different facades of the problem, a different perspective can emerge. Many times, there are factors in a difficult situation that we are not aware of. By pausing, reflecting, and praying a calmer more measured response may develop.

Pray
Hold my hand in Weakness.
Loving God, you are my strength. Hold my hand in my weakness and teach my heart to fly. With you, there's nothing to fear, nothing to worry about. Hold me tight in your embrace, so that I can be stronger than the challenges in my life.

Friday

David and Goliath
1 Samuel 17

32 David said to Saul, "Let no one lose heart on account of this Philistine; your servant will go and fight him."

33 Saul replied, "You are not able to go out against this Philistine and fight him; you are only a young man, and he has been a warrior from his youth."

34 But David said to Saul, "Your servant has been keeping his father's sheep. When a lion or a bear came and carried off a sheep from the flock, 35 I went after it, struck it, and rescued the sheep from its mouth. When it turned on me, I seized it by its hair, struck it and killed it. 36 Your servant has killed both the lion and the bear; this uncircumcised Philistine will be like one of them, because he has defied the armies of the living God. 37 The Lord who rescued me from the paw of the lion and the paw of the bear will rescue me from the hand of this Philistine."

Saul said to David, "Go, and the Lord be with you."

38 Then Saul dressed David in his own tunic. He put a coat of armour on him and a bronze helmet on his head. 39 David fastened on his sword over the tunic and tried walking around, because he was not used to them.

"I cannot go in these," he said to Saul, "because I am not used to them." So, he took them off.

40 Then he took his staff in his hand, chose five smooth stones from the stream, put them in the pouch of his shepherd's bag and, with his sling in his hand, approached the Philistine.

In 'David and Goliath: Underdogs, Misfits, and the Art of Battling Giants,' Malcolm Gladwell discusses David's advantages.

David was not used to wearing heavy armour. He knew it would slow him down. David was aware of what would defeat him. *His strength was his speed.*

David's sling was a devastating weapon. It's one of the most feared weapons in the ancient world. The stone that came from his sling had the stopping power equivalent to a bullet from a pistol. It was a serious weapon.

David did have the upper hand. It is because of, and not despite, David's size and unorthodox choice of weapon that he is able to face down the giant. *In other words, Gladwell says, most people underestimate the importance of their own gifts.*

Lent Spiritual Prompt

Assess your own gifts and abilities, and how God can use them.

Pray

Lord, I come to ask for your healing, teach me of your love; I reveal to you all of my unspoken fears and shame.

Take my selfish thoughts and actions, the petty feuds, please hear me now appealing to you. Teach me of your love.

Soothe away my pain and sorrow, hold me in love. Your grace I cannot buy or borrow, hold me in your love.

Though I see but dark and danger, though I spurn both friend and stranger, though I often dread tomorrow, hold me in your love.

Make the faith that I have in you more than just an empty token, fill me with your love. Help me live for others, please bind me in your love.

Show me what talents I have and how I can use them for you.

Saturday

David and Goliath
1 Samuel 17

41 Meanwhile, the Philistine, with his shield bearer in front of him, kept coming closer to David. 42 He looked David over and saw that he was little more than a boy, glowing with health and handsome, and he despised him. 43 He said to David, "Am I a dog, that you come at me with sticks?" And the Philistine cursed David by his gods. 44 "Come here," he said, "and I'll give your flesh to the birds and the wild animals!"

45 David said to the Philistine, "You come against me with sword, spear, and javelin, but I come against you in the name of the Lord Almighty, the God of the armies of Israel, whom you have defied. 46 This day the Lord will deliver you into my hands, and I'll strike you down and cut off your head. This very day I will give the carcasses of the Philistine army to the birds and the wild animals, and the whole world will know that there is a God in Israel. 47 All those gathered here will know that it is not by sword or spear that the Lord saves; for the battle is the Lord's, and he will give all of you into our hands."

48 As the Philistine moved closer to attack him, David ran quickly toward the battle line to meet him. 49 Reaching into his bag and taking out a stone, he slung it and struck the Philistine on the forehead. The stone sank into his forehead, and he fell face down on the ground.

50 So David triumphed over the Philistine with a sling and a stone; without a sword in his hand, he struck down the Philistine and killed him.

51 David ran and stood over him. He took hold of the Philistine's sword and drew it from the sheath. After he killed him, he cut off his head with the sword.

When the Philistines saw that their hero was dead, they turned and ran. 52 Then the men of Israel and Judah surged forward with a shout and pursued the Philistines to the entrance of Gath and to the gates of Ekron. Their dead were strewn along the Shaaraim road to Gath and Ekron. 53 When the Israelites returned from chasing the Philistines, they plundered their camp.

54 David took the Philistine's head and brought it to Jerusalem; he put the Philistine's weapons in his own tent.

55 As Saul watched David going out to meet the Philistine, he said to Abner, commander of the army, "Abner, whose son is that young man?"

Abner replied, "As surely as you live, Your Majesty, I don't know."

56 The king said, "Find out whose son this young man is."

57 As soon as David returned from killing the Philistine, Abner took him and brought him before Saul, with David still holding the Philistine's head.

58 "Whose son are you, young man?" Saul asked him.

David said, "I am the son of your servant Jesse of Bethlehem."

Contrary to the traditional view of giant versus boy, another view of David and Goliath is that there is a big lumbering man weighed down with armour, who can't see much more than a few feet in front of his face, up against a boy running at him with a devastating weapon and a rock travelling with the stopping power of a handgun. In this interpretation it is Goliath who was the vulnerable one. The only way he could have beaten David was by literally getting his hands on him – but David had no need to go anywhere near him. David had a sling.

This is not a story of an underdog. David has numerous advantages in that battle, but they are not initially obvious.

Ancient armies contained teams of slingers, who could be deadly from distances as great as 200 yards. The best, like David, were lethally accurate, and Goliath was not a small target. Once David had persuaded the Israelites that single combat did not have to be sword versus sword, but could be a sling, then the dynamics completely changed.

The strong are often surprisingly weak, if looked at from the right angle. People who seem weak can turn out to be surprisingly strong.

With the right training, we could all beat Goliath – but David was the only one who spotted how to win and had the courage to break with convention, everyone else assumed they had to fight Goliath with a sword.

In our own life we need to do a better job of looking for an advantage during a crisis.

Although there maybe obstacles and obstructions in our life, we should look at what advantages these barriers can bring. Remember crisis brings change and sometimes, although it is not what we want, it may be what we need and what is best for us.

Pray

Loving God, thank you for all your good gifts to me. Help me to recognise the advantages in the difficult situation I am enduring. Grant me wisdom and acceptance.

- **Fourth Week of Lent**

Sunday

Lord Jesus Christ, Son of God, have mercy on me, a sinner.

This short prayer is often called the Jesus Prayer. Pray it a few times a day and it starts burrowing into your soul. It is an old prayer. The prayer is said, slowly, rhythmically, again and again. And it just . . . stays with you.

Lord Jesus Christ, Son of God, have mercy on me, a sinner.

Like all prayers used regularly, it is an invitation to learn to inhabit the words, to let them seep into the soul and fashion us into the likeness of Christ.

Lord Jesus Christ, Son of God, have mercy on me, a sinner.

It brings us face to face with God, and with ourselves. It is because God is all-powerful and all-loving, both at once and in equal measure, that we can come before God as we are, without fear, knowing that our prayers and requests will be heard gently and compassionately.

Lord Jesus Christ, Son of God, have mercy on me, a sinner.

"Have mercy" is a cry that resonates throughout our scriptures. It is the cry of those who beg, those who are hurt, those who are rejected in the Gospels. It is the cry of the people of Israel throughout the Old Testament. Often, they do not even cry out to God, but simply cry out or groan in pain. God sees, God hears, and God has compassion.

Lord Jesus Christ, Son of God, have mercy on me, a sinner.

It is compassion that shapes God's response to a broken world. There is no need to tell God what to do; no need to offer elaborate solutions; no need to bargain. The prayer is not verbose: what we need is for God's mercy and compassion to transform us and our world.

Lord Jesus Christ, Son of God, have mercy on me, a sinner.

We struggle with knowing ourselves fully. We feel guilt and shame for things that are not our responsibility, while failing to notice the things that are. Simply asking for mercy makes a generous space into which to bring the whole of ourselves and invite the Spirit to work within us in ways that we may not be able to foresee, understand, or put into words.

Lord Jesus Christ, Son of God, have mercy on me, a sinner.

Ultimately, this is a prayer of trust, that God will know how to answer the cry of our hearts when all we can say is "Lord Jesus Christ, Son of God, have mercy on me, a sinner."

Monday

Intentional Praying

We all have important relationships in our lives, relationships that matter and make a difference to who we are and how we live. Unfortunately, it can be easy to go through our days and weeks forgetting to pray for those people in our lives. One helpful way to change this is to be intentional about praying through our important relationships, like Paul was. Paul said in his letter to the Philippian church in Philippians 1:3-4,

I give thanks to my God for every remembrance of you, always praying with joy for all of you in my every prayer.

This Lent allow time each day to pray through your important relationships. Make a list.

Pray for those important relationships now.

Tuesday

James 2:14-17
What good is it, my brothers, if someone says he has faith but does not have works? Can that faith save him? If a brother or sister is poorly clothed and lacking in daily food, and one of you says to them, "Go in peace, be warmed and filled," without giving them the things needed for the body, what good is that? So also, faith by itself if it does not have works, is dead.

Some people who are without a home feel distraught and heartbroken, they feel forgotten in today's world. Praying for the homeless brings their troubles and needs directly to God. We all have the opportunity to pray for the homeless.

Pray

Mighty God, You are the giver of every good and perfect gift. Thank You for the resources to aid those without homes and those who are hungry.

Empower those who serve and multiply their efforts, so no one goes without. I pray for those who are distraught and heartbroken. Draw close to them and bless them with your peace.

Gratitude

How Can I Be Kind?

The Lord's Prayer

Our Father, who art in heaven,
hallowed be thy name;
thy kingdom come;
thy will be done;
on earth as it is in heaven.
Give us this day our daily bread.
And forgive us our trespasses,
as we forgive those who trespass
against us.
And lead us not into temptation;
but deliver us from evil.
For thine is the kingdom,
the power and the glory,
for ever an ever
Amen

Rewrite the Lord's Prayer, putting it into your own words. Add any phrases that help you express each petition in terms of your own circumstances. Try praying your version of the Lord's Prayer for seven days. Feel free to revise the wording as you discover new ways to express this ancient prayer in a personal way.

Prayer Challenge:

Over the few weeks write down the 'daily bread' needs you have asked God for. Then look back and think about how God has answered your prayers.

Take a moment to pray for your own needs, the needs of your family, friends, as well as those of your church.

Answers to Prayer

Wednesday

Giving

Even a seemingly small act of generosity can grow into something far beyond what we could ever ask or imagine (Eph. 3:20)

— the creation of a community of love in this world, and beyond this world, because wherever love grows, it is stronger than death (1 Cor. 13:8).

So, when we give ourselves to planting and nurturing love here on earth, our efforts will reach out beyond our own chronological existence. Indeed, if we raise funds for the creation of a community of love, we are helping God build the kingdom. We are doing exactly what we are supposed to do as Christians. Paul is clear about this: 'Make love your aim' (1 Cor. 14:1).

'We accept the call to be deeply, deeply connected with unconditional love, with our own fragile humanity, and with people everywhere.' – Henri Nouwen 1932-1996

Message from the Rector

We believe there has never been a more important time to build communities of faith that are open-hearted and open-minded, committed to service of others and determined to work across faiths for the good of all. St James's has for decades, tried to build that kind of community, where compassion and imagination are placed at the service of the common good. Our ambition is high, not for ourselves, but for our city and society, most especially for those in need or trouble of any kind. We want to be part of building a London that all of us want to live In. And for us, this means remaining faithful to our purpose: to be a place, even in the middle of the city, of peaceful contemplation, just action, environmental sustainability, and lively debate. We simply couldn't fulfil our purpose without your support. It's only thanks to you that we are able to do what we do. And if there are ways in which we can help you, please don't hesitate to let us know.

Thank you.

With very best wishes,

[signature]

Rev Lucy Winkett
Rector, St James's Church, Piccadilly

Pray
Loving God, there are so many people in need and so many people willing to help. Please direct me in your ways so that I can help.

Thursday

1 Peter 5:6–7
Humble yourselves, therefore, under the mighty hand of God so that at the proper time He may exalt you, casting all your anxieties on Him, because He cares for you.

Jonathan Haidt, the social psychologist, in his essay: "Why the Past 10 Years of American Life Have Been Uniquely Stupid" argues that social media is having a devastating impact on society. He invokes the parable of the Tower of Babel, in which God, "offended by the hubris of humanity," makes the people unable to communicate.

Haidt's position is that "Our institutions are malfunctioning because of the way that social media amplifies performance, moralism and mob dynamics, which brings the normal process of dissent to a grinding halt."

Haidt believes that social media has armed us with "darts," which he describes as "attempts to shame or punish someone publicly while broadcasting one's own virtue, brilliance or tribal loyalties." These darts cause "pain but no fatalities" yet are enough to have had a chilling effect on discourse. This has resulted in institutions having a "chronic fear of getting darted," thus making them "stupider."

Our culture today elevates image, self-promotion, and keeping up appearances. So, we exchange our real and authentic selves for a hyped-up, glamorised, and airbrushed caricature of ourselves. We become someone else. Our culture celebrates pleasure. So, we avoid pain at all costs, stuff it down, numb it, hide it, and ignore it, believing that it has nothing to teach us. Our culture celebrates perfection. So, we strive to make the grade, have a good bank balance, and a recognisable name. Jesus comes and overturns the self-promotion, fake tables. He sets us free from the straight jacket of social media. He gives us forgiveness to be ourselves, to be accepted for who we are.

Pray
Loving God please forgive me if I have 'darted' anyone. Show me how to make amends. Dear God, you know the times that I have been hurt. Show me if it was just my pride and ego that was darted or if it was deeper, please heal this pain I carry around.

Friday

Psalm 140:12
I know that the Lord will maintain the cause of the afflicted and will execute justice for the needy.

Proverbs 19:17
Whoever is generous to the poor lends to the Lord, and he will repay him for his deed.

God listens to our prayers. We may not know the outcome of our prayers. Yet, we do know those prayers are heard. God's plan is working through each situation and in every moment.

When we open our hearts, minds, and souls, and seek to have a conversation with the Lord, we are drawing close to Him.

Pray

Dearest God, I come before You with a heart full of gratitude for Your loving care and boundless grace. Thank You for the countless blessings You have showered upon me, despite my unworthiness. I lift up my brothers and sisters who are without homes or employment. I pray they may be clothed in Your armour, protected by Your shield, and strengthened by Your love. Please provide work and shelter for them.

Saturday

Colossians 2 :6-7
As you therefore have received Christ Jesus the Lord, so walk in Him, rooted, and built up in Him and established in the faith, as you have been taught, abounding in it with thanksgiving.

Isaiah12:4-5
And on that day, you will say, "Give thanks to the LORD, call on His name. Make known His deeds among the peoples; make them remember that His name is exalted." Praise the LORD in song, for He has done glorious things; let this be known throughout the earth.

Pray
Loving God, I praise your name.

You are my God, who longs to heal and reconcile, who holds me in faithfulness, thank you, God.

You are my God, please make me in this time of Lent a hearer and doer of your word, lead me as I follow Jesus in his journey in the desert, in my journey to wholeness, forgiveness, healing, and grace.

Giving & Receiving

People To Pray For

Lord Help Me

How can I serve God better?

Father, I pray about this situation ...

- **Fifth Week of Lent**

Sunday

Romans 5:3-5
3 Not only so, but we also glory in our sufferings, because we know that suffering produces perseverance; 4 perseverance, character; and character, hope. 5 And hope does not put us to shame, because God's love has been poured out into our hearts through the Holy Spirit, who has been given to us.

Lent is a time when we are encouraged to turn to God and God's word in the Bible and allow it to be reflected in our own lives to enable us to see ourselves as we really are.

This Lent, let our focus be on the Christ who for our sakes was humble and obedient to his heavenly Father even to the point of suffering and dying for our sakes, and – as Jesus was obedient let us too, seek to be obedient to God's call on us and on our lives.

Breathe into me, Holy Spirit, that my thoughts may all be holy. Move in me, Holy Spirit, that my work, too, may be holy. Attract my heart, Holy Spirit, that I may love only what is holy. Strengthen me, Holy Spirit, that I may defend all that is holy. Protect me, Holy Spirit, that I may always be holy. Saint Augustine

Pray
My Dearest Jesus, Today, I want to be a light for you. Shine your love into my heart so that I may reflect that love to every person that I encounter. Amen

End of the day

Lord God, I give You unending thanks, for You have brought me once again to the end of another day. I am grateful that I have seen yet another day pass, and You have kept me and blessed me from sunrise to sunset. Continue to bless me during the night and continue to guide my steps each day of my life.

Monday

The Fast Life

Fast from judging others.
Feast on Christ.
Fast from fear of illness.
Feast on the healing power of God.
Fast from words that pollute.
Feast on speech that purifies.
Fast from discontent.
Feast on gratitude.
Fast from anger.
Feast on patience.
Fast from pessimism.
Feast on hope.
Fast from negatives.
Feast on encouragement.
Fast from bitterness.
Feast on forgiveness.
Fast from self-concern.
Feast on compassion.
Fast from suspicion.
Feast on truth.
Fast from gossip.
Feast on purposeful silence.
Fast from problems that overwhelm.
Feast on prayer that sustains.
Fast from anxiety.
Feast on faith.

Changes Going Forward

Can you think of a time when you wanted vengeance or retribution towards someone who wronged you? How did it make you feel? Did you tell God about it? Pray about it now?

Tuesday

Philippians 4:4-7
Rejoice in the Lord always. I will say it again: Rejoice! Let your gentleness be evident to all. The Lord is near. Do not be anxious about anything, but in every situation, by prayer and petition, with thanksgiving, present your requests to God. And the peace of God, which transcends all understanding, will guard your hearts and your minds in Christ Jesus.

At any time, some people can suffer spikes of anxiety and sadness. If this is you, then pray for God's peace and calmness to descend upon you. If it is not you, pray for others who are suffering.

Pray
Loving God, please draw close to me and grant me your peace to my troubled thoughts and anxiety. Teach me to rely on You and not to be anxious about anything. I pray for others who are suffering from melancholy. Please ease their pain.

Wednesday

Mark 2:13-17
Jesus went out again beside the lake; the whole crowd gathered around him, and he taught them. As he was walking along, he saw Levi son of Alphaeus sitting at the tax booth, and he said to him, 'Follow me.' And he got up and followed him. And as he sat at dinner in Levi's house, many tax-collectors and sinners were also sitting with Jesus and his disciples—for there were many who followed him. When the scribes of the Pharisees saw that he was eating with sinners and tax collectors, they said to his disciples, 'Why does he eat with tax-collectors and sinners?' When Jesus heard this, he said to them, 'Those who are well have no need of a physician, but those who are sick do; I have come to call not the righteous but sinners.'

How might this story from Mark's Gospel connect with the theme of hospitality and belonging?
Who is the host? Who is the guest?
Why might that be important?
How and why might this passage connect and resonate with:
- You
- Your Church
- The World
What does belonging feel like?
What does it look like?
How can we create a culture of belonging at your Church?
Why does this matter?

Pray
Dear God, show me that I belong. Thank you for giving me people who I can have fellowship with. Please let me look around to those who feel they don't belong and give me the courage to offer them the hand of fellowship.

Thursday

Philippians 4:12-13
I know how to be brought low, and I know how to abound. In any and every circumstance, I have learned the secret of facing plenty and hunger, abundance and need. I can do all things through him who strengthens me.

What do you chase in life? Is it control: the feeling that nothing, within reason, has the power to overwhelm you.

Remember that crisis brings change and sometimes change is required. We may not be able to control what is beyond us, but we can control how we react to crisis and change.

Lent Spiritual Prompt
What do you feel God wants you to change in your life?
Reflection on a recent situation when you felt God's presence.

Pray
Gracious God you know every aspect of my life. Even the number of hairs on my head. These things that are happening in the world and in my life are making me anxious. Please grant me your peace. Ever-loving God, I confess that I have sinned in thought, word, and deed. I have not loved you with my whole heart. I have not loved my neighbours as myself. In your mercy forgive what I have been, help me to amend what I am, and direct what I shall be, that I may do justly, love mercy, and walk humbly with you, my God. Amen.

Friday

Thessalonians 5:16-18
Rejoice always, pray continually, give thanks in all circumstances; for this is God's will for you in Christ Jesus.

From the Beginning of Time
Jesus, you have known us from the beginning of time.
Jesus, you have known us in the depths of our dreams and in the darkness of our shame, you know us as your beloved.

Help us to own that core identity more and more in this season of repentance and mercy.

Give us the rock-solid assurance of your unwavering faith in us as we seek you.

When our life is at its strongest. When our days are at their longest, Kyrie eleison, Lord have mercy.

At the first coming of the dawn, on the life that's newly born, Kyrie eleison, Lord have mercy.

At the turning of the tide, on life's ocean deep and wide, Kyrie eleison, Lord have mercy.

When our powers are nearly done, at the setting of the sun, Kyrie eleison, Lord have mercy.

When we come to breathe our last, when the gates of death are passed, Kyrie eleison, Lord have mercy.

Pray

God of heaven and earth, as Jesus taught his disciples to be persistent in prayer, give me patience and courage never to lose hope, but always to bring my prayers before you, through Jesus Christ our Lord.

Saturday

John 14:27
"Peace, I leave with you; my peace I give you. I do not give to you as the world gives. Do not let your hearts be troubled and do not be afraid."

Pray

God of miracles and wonder. For whom nothing is impossible. You long to reveal yourself to me. That I might reach out to you. I know myself to be your own. Cherished and chosen.

Forgive me, if I have been too preoccupied and distracted to notice the extraordinary in the ordinary.

Forgive me, if I have failed to recognise you in the faces of both friends and strangers. Forgive me Father, if I have let the sound of my own voice drown out your call.

What is God saying to me?

Lent Reflections

Prayer List

Answers to Prayer

Holy Week

- **Holy Week**

Holy Week is a significant time of remembrance of the life, death, and resurrection of Jesus. The week begins on Palm Sunday, commemorating Jesus' triumphant entry into Jerusalem, and ends on Easter Sunday, celebrating His resurrection.

Holy Week is a time of Spiritual reflection as we think about what Jesus' life, death, and resurrection means to us personally. It is also a time to focus on the teachings of Jesus and strive to live a life that reflects His teachings.

Palm Sunday

There is a saying: 'The first step is the hardest...' Have you ever found this? Especially if the journey is a difficult one; one that you don't really want to do perhaps, or one that is scary or unpleasant. Jesus stands on the Mount of Olives, overlooking the walled city of Jerusalem and the Temple. He knows what is ahead - 'We are going up to Jerusalem,' he tells his disciples in Matthew 20:18; 'and the Son of Man will be delivered over to the chief priests and the teachers of the law. They will condemn him to death and will hand him over to the Gentiles to be mocked and flogged and crucified.'

The Mount of Olives looks one way over Jerusalem but turn the other way and the view is over the Judaean Wilderness to the Dead Sea and, beyond that, Jordan. Jesus could have fled. He could have gone back into the wilderness. No one would have found him. Yet he doesn't. He takes the first step on what he knows will be a difficult journey. He tells his disciples to go find a donkey - fulfilling prophecies made so many years before - and takes his first steps down towards Jerusalem, towards pain, betrayal, and death.

Why? Why does he take such a hard road?
Because he knows what lies beyond the pain and the death - life.
Matthew 20:18 'On the third day he will be raised to life.'

This Palm Sunday we start our walk with Christ through Holy Week, through the sorrow of Good Friday to the joy of Easter Sunday.

In ancient times, palm branches were a symbol of victory and triumph. They were often used to celebrate military victories or to welcome royalty. When Jesus rode into Jerusalem on a donkey in John 12, the crowds saw Him as a king, and they welcomed Him with palm branches as a symbol of His triumphal entry into the city.

As we reflect on Palm Sunday, we can consider the way we welcome Jesus into our own lives. Do we welcome Him as King, or do we sometimes push Him aside in favour of other things? Are we willing to follow Jesus wherever He leads us, or only when it is comfortable or convenient?

Pray

Holy Week

Creator God, during this Holy Week, you invite me into a time of conversion and reflection upon my relationship to others. My caring for others is a great joy, but also a grave responsibility and there are times when I feel that I shall stumble under its weight.

As I begin Holy Week, I ask you to draw near and be with me. In my conversations with others may I come to a richer understanding of the common good of all creation that you have asked me to guard. Deepen my appreciation for both human dignity and human limits. Guide me in your service.

Gracious God, I praise you for Jesus Christ who entered the heart of Jerusalem to shouts of "Hosanna" that first Palm Sunday. May I, too, invite Christ into the hidden places of my heart. As I remember the sorrow and suffering of our Saviour this week, deepen my faith and teach me to rejoice in his ultimate victory. Amen

Monday

Journeys are not just about getting from A to B. When we go for a walk with friends, it is the talking and listening to each other which brings usually more joy than the walk itself.

Faith is a journey with God. But what happens if we don't feel like we are hearing from him?

John 12:29 "Then a voice came from heaven, 'I have glorified it, and will glorify it again.' The crowd that was there and heard it said that it thundered; others said an angel had spoken to him. Jesus said, 'This voice was for your benefit, not mine.'

Some of us might hear God loud and clear, like thunder. For others it might be a whisper. For some we may not hear anything verbally, but know the voice of God through the words of others, or the words of

Scripture.

However, those who heard God's voice - whether as thunder or as the voice of an angel - heard it because they were there, listening. As we journey with Jesus this week, let's put some time aside to listen.

Choose a piece of music to listen to that best reflects the mood you wish to feel. Set aside time to listen to it in comfort, perhaps resting in a bed or a cosy chair, with a candle, picture or cross to focus on as you listen.

Pray
Heavenly Father, I wait upon you. I pause, still my mind and still my heart. I wait upon you. I stop and listen beyond the everyday. I wait upon you. I rest and allow my soul to have space. I wait upon you. Quiet, at rest, held. I wait upon you.

Tuesday

John 12:3 'Then Mary took about half a litre of pure nard, and expensive perfume; she poured it on
Jesus' feet and wiped his feet with her hair.'

In the presence of others (her family and the disciples) Mary lets down her hair (a definite social no-no), bends down, and gets far closer to Jesus than any social etiquette of the day allowed. She broke the rules of propriety, and she broke the rules of modesty.
She wasted all that wonderful perfume.
Or did she?
Why do you think she did it?
Why do you think she risked the scorn of her family? Of her friends? Of Jesus' friends? And even of Jesus himself?
Jesus rebukes Judas when Judas scorns Mary's actions. Why?
'You will not always have me.'

On the cross Jesus pours out everything for us.
On the cross his life is poured out so that we may have life.
On the cross Jesus breaks the rules of life and death - dying, and then

rising again.

In your house find something that smells wonderful - some perfume perhaps, or a
scented candle, a flower, or even some food.
Enjoy the fragrance and remember the presence of Christ with you.

Pray
Gracious God, I know you have searched me, and you know me. I know you are the beginning and the end. I know you are the Redeemer. I wait upon you, allowing your grace to engulf my whole being. And in this place, close, protected and eternal I find that this grace renews my strength, wipes away my tears, and promises new hope. I wait upon you.

Wednesday

John 13:18 Jesus Predicts His Betrayal
18 "I am not referring to all of you; I know those I have chosen. But this is to fulfil this passage of Scripture: 'He who shared my bread has turned against me.'

19 "I am telling you now before it happens, so that when it does happen you will believe that I am who I am. 20 Very truly I tell you, whoever accepts anyone I send accepts me; and whoever accepts me accepts the one who sent me."

21 After he had said this, Jesus was troubled in spirit and testified, "Very truly I tell you, one of you is going to betray me."

22 His disciples stared at one another, at a loss to know which of them he meant. 23 One of them, the disciple whom Jesus loved, was reclining next to him. 24 Simon Peter motioned to this disciple and said, "Ask him which one he means."

25 Leaning back against Jesus, he asked him, "Lord, who is it?"

26 Jesus answered, "It is the one to whom I will give this piece of bread when I have dipped it in the dish." Then, dipping the piece of bread, he gave it to Judas, the son of Simon Iscariot. 27 As soon as Judas took the bread, Satan entered into him.

So, Jesus told him, "What you are about to do, do quickly." 28 But no one at the meal understood why Jesus said this to him. 29 Since Judas had charge of the money, some thought Jesus was telling him to buy what was needed for the festival, or to give something to the poor. 30 As soon as Judas had taken the bread, he went out. And it was night.

We have so much to learn from Jesus' behaviour.
We, too, will have been betrayed in our lives, treated unjustly, hurt, talked about, the subject of gossip. It hurts, and that pain can linger.
How do we respond to those who hurt us?
How could, or should we respond?
What prevents us from acting with dignity, empathy and ultimately forgiveness?

Take a piece of bread and a small bowl with a little oil or melted butter in. Remember the times when you've felt betrayed and pray as you feel able for healing and peace, for all involved. Dip your bread into the bowl and remember that we have hurt others, and they have hurt us, often unintentionally. Eat and know that – through Christ – we can forgive and be forgiven.

Maundy Thursday

Maundy Thursday - the day when we remember how Jesus washed the feet of his disciples. Peter doesn't get the lesson, first refusing to let Jesus wash his feet, because that is not what a
respected person with authority does, and then wanting to jump right in and be washed from head to toe. He thought the lesson was about purity. But it wasn't.
It was about humility.

John 13:13   Jesus Washes His Disciples' Feet
...13 You call Me Teacher and Lord, and rightly so, because I am. 14 So if I, your Lord, and Teacher, have washed your feet, you also

should wash one another's feet. 15 I have set you an example so that you should do as I have done for you....

To wash another's feet is a humbling task. There is no getting away from it - people's feet can be smelly at the best of times.

It is also humbling to have your feet washed by others.

How do we serve one another?
How do we let others serve us?
Does a lack of humility ever stop us from helping others, or indeed, letting others help us?

Pray
Think of those who have helped you and thank God for them.
Think of those you have helped - and thank God you were able to help them.
Ask God - who else may I help? May I have the humility to help them?

Good Friday

Luke 23:34 When Jesus hung on the cross, He prayed for His persecutors, "Father, forgive them; for they know not what they do.

Back on Palm Sunday we talked about Jesus starting his journey towards Jerusalem - a journey that he knew would end here: on the cross.
It was a lonely journey.

A friend betrayed him.
A friend denied knowing him.
His other friends fled in fear.

In the space of a few days Jesus went from being cheered into the gates of Jerusalem, showered with palm leaves and the cheers of the crowd…to being on his own, alone and abandoned, on the cross.

Only, if we look closely at the story, we see that he wasn't alone, not completely. His mother, Mary, was with him, as was Mary the wife of Clopas, and Mary Magdalene. They couldn't be right next to him, but they were as close as they could be.

Then, with his dying breath he said 'It is finished' - restoring the relationship between humans and their God, which had been broken ever since Adam and Eve ate the fruit in the Garden of Eden.

This Good Friday, why not contact someone who might be feeling alone; or contact someone who you have not spoken to in a while.

The crucifixion of Jesus on Good Friday serves as a reminder of the suffering that Jesus endured for our salvation. During Good Friday we take time to remember the sacrifice Jesus made and His great love for us.

Pray

Give thanks that we have a God who knows what it is to be alone yet promises to be with us always.

Pray for your persecutors.
Ask God for strength to forgive them.

Give thanks for the sacrifice Jesus made for you and for his great love for you.

Prayer Requests

Lenten Reflections

Saturday

Luke 9:2   Whoever wishes to be my follower must deny his very self, take up his cross each day, and follow in my steps."

John 1:5 'The light shines in the darkness, and the darkness has not overcome it.'

We don't often stop to consider the significance of that silent Saturday.

Saturday is that middle day when God occupied a grave in a garden outside of Jerusalem.

Saturday is a day to reflect on the in-between moments of our own lives. It's a day to sit, to wait, to hope, even when we're unsure of what tomorrow will bring.

We can look back and know now that Easter comes on Sunday, but Jesus' followers didn't know that back then.

When we feel hopeless, lost, confused, or grieving, we can remember that Jesus' followers know exactly how that feels.

Saturday is about the hard and uncertain days that God still calls holy.

Take sometime today just to sit.

Pray for those who feel lost, who feel without hope.

People In Need

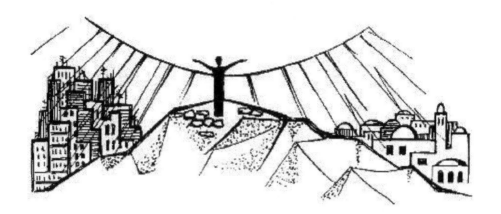

Happy Easter
REJOICE
Christ has risen.

The impossible has happened – Jesus is risen, death has been defeated! No longer do we have to carry the guilt of our wrongdoings. We are loved and accepted, despite our flaws; if we turn our eyes to the risen Christ, we are washed clean and forgiven.

Alleluia! Alleluia!

Our Lord is Risen! He is Risen indeed!

By his great mercy God has given us new birth into a living hope, through the resurrection of Jesus from the dead, and into an inheritance which cannot perish or be defiled, nor can it ever fade. So let us rejoice!

If you can, spend some time outside in a garden, or near some flowers, or on a walk; enjoy all that God has given you, and rejoice.

Bible Verses

Prayer List

Lessons of Lent

Changes Made in Lent

PRAYER CHALLENGE:

Reflect on how God has challenged you over the last few months.

If you have kept a prayer diary, look back through it and see what He has said to you.

Looking Back Over Lent

Giving & Receiving

Changes to carry on after Lent?

Prayers Answered

---o0o---

Feedback
If you have constructive feedback or wish to make contributions to further Lent books, please email the Publishers at lentjournal@gmail.com

Have a look at the other Lent Publication books on Amazon including the Lent books and Prayer Books and Journals.

Please consider leaving a positive review on Amazon as this will bring this book to the attention of more Christians.

Thank you and God bless You.

---o0o---

Blessing
May God who established the dance of creation, who marvelled at the lilies of the field, who transforms chaos to order, lead us to transform our lives and the Church.
May the God who made all that is, forgive you and set you free.
May you take God's forgiveness to heart and be at peace.
And the blessing of God: Creator, Christ and Holy Spirit be with you this Easter and remain with you on this day and for ever.
Amen.

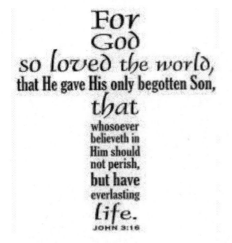

For God so loved the world, that He gave His only begotten Son, that whosoever believeth in Him should not perish, but have everlasting life.
JOHN 3:16

Printed in Great Britain
by Amazon